BRITAIN IN OLD PHOTOGRAPHS

RICHMOND
PAST & PRESENT

JOHN CLOAKE

New Photographs by
Graham Fletcher and Shelley Churchman

SUTTON PUBLISHING LIMITED

Sutton Publishing Limited
Phoenix Mill · Thrupp · Stroud
Gloucestershire · GL5 2BU

First published 1999
Reprinted 2006

British Library Cataloguing in Publication Data
A catalogue record for this book is available from the
British Library

ISBN 0-7509-1842-X

Typeset in 10.5/13.5 Photina.
Typesetting and origination by
Sutton Publishing Limited.
Printed and bound in the USA.

Buses passing on Richmond Bridge 1913 and 1995 – a montage of the photographs on page 90.

CONTENTS

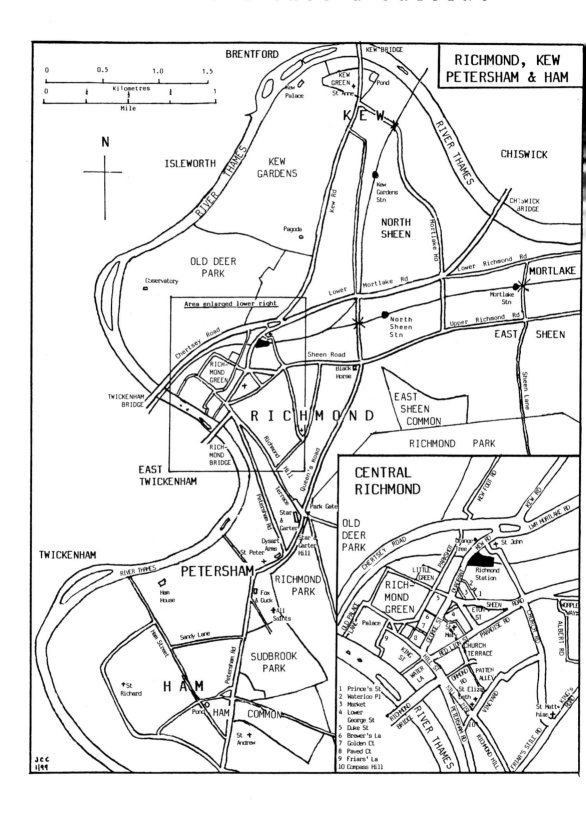

RICHMOND, KEW
PETERSHAM & HAM

INTRODUCTION

In January 1996 the Museum of Richmond mounted a temporary exhibition showing side by side some thirty old photographs of the Richmond area and up-to-date views of the same scenes – specially taken to be closely matched to the originals. The exhibition was a popular success and many people expressed the hope that these comparison views might in due course be published in book form.

This book takes its inspiration and starting point from that exhibition. Nearly all of the photographs then shown are included in it, but to that nucleus have now been added more than twice as many again. The geographical coverage, as for the exhibition, is limited to the former Borough of Richmond – Richmond itself, Kew, Petersham and Ham. The views are arranged in a rough north–south sequence, from Kew to Ham. Some of the old and new contrasts show total rebuilding; others show little alteration in the buildings and topography but a striking change in the context: in traffic, roadsigns, people, trees.

The 'old' photographs are not all of one period. One or two are relatively recent, such as those showing the riverside site before the large-scale development of the 1980s. Most, however, are at least fifty years old, many are about a hundred years old, and a few close to a hundred and fifty. In a few cases it has been possible to produce 'triplets' to show three periods of development. Some of the old photographs may be familiar, having already been published in *Richmond in Old Photographs* or similar books, though many others are published here for the first time. For the purposes of this book it did not seem right to exclude good photographs which presented interesting opportunities for modern-day comparisons merely because they had been used before.

In general the photographs of Richmond present have been matched as closely as possible to their predecessors of Richmond past, by viewpoint and angle of shot, by season, time of day and weather conditions – and sometimes even by traffic and people. There are, however, a few exceptions, if only for the sake of variety. Where little or nothing of the old is recognizable in the new the photographers have allowed themselves more licence – presenting in two cases even night scenes instead of daytime ones, though from the same point. On occasion the growth of trees has been such as to block out entirely what was the focal point in the old photograph, requiring a change of season in the new one so that the buildings in question might be visible through almost bare branches. In a few cases modern road traffic has compelled a slight alteration of viewpoint: where Victorian photographers could set up their tripods in the middle of an almost empty road, their successors today cannot even step off the pavement in safety. And while those Victorian photographers would often try to ensure that there should be no intruders whose movements might blur their long exposures or would carefully group a few static onlookers, our present-day photographers have been happy to include the people who live in or visit these scenes today.

The source of most of the old photographs used is the local studies collection of the Richmond Public Library and the authors are most grateful to the Council of the London Borough of Richmond upon Thames for permission to reproduce them. Very grateful thanks are due to Jane Baxter, the Librarian in charge of the collection, for her most effective help in tracing and selecting photographs. It is good to know that this splendid archive collection – many of the pictures presented by the keen amateur photographers of Richmond some hundred years ago – is to be matched by a new collection aiming to record every street, and indeed house, in the Borough as a millennium project. Let us hope that this will form a basis for a new 'Past and Present' book in another hundred years' time.

A few items come from the author's own collection. One is from the Chiswick Public Library. Thanks are also expressed to Sylvia Greenwood for lending two pictures of Ham for copying. Two other photographs, reproduced from a previous publication, came from private collections whose owners are now untraceable.

C H A P T E R   O N E

KEW

The first wooden bridge at Kew (above) was built in 1759 by Robert Tunstall, proprietor of the ferry which it replaced. This engraving was published in that year. (Author's collection)

Kew grew up as a little hamlet at the Surrey end of an important ford across the Thames from Brentford. The name, originally Cay-ho, is of Anglo-Saxon derivation, but the first historical mention of Kew comes in the early fourteenth century, when five of the land-holding tenants of the manor of Shene lived there. Most of the meadows and woodlands of the manor were at Kew.

The hamlet came into prominence in Tudor times when several grandees of the royal court had mansions there – conveniently close to the royal palace at Richmond (as Henry VII had renamed Shene). A small village gradually developed around the sides of Kew Green. In 1728 Queen Caroline leased property there to extend the royal Richmond estate. In 1731 Frederick Prince of Wales acquired a house on the south side of the western extremity of the Green, which subsequently became the summer home of George III and Queen Charlotte. The botanic garden started by Prince Frederick and his wife Augusta became the nucleus of the Royal Botanic Gardens of today.

The second Kew Bridge in the 1890s. The wooden bridge was replaced in 1783–9 by a new stone one, sited a hundred feet or so further east. It was designed by James Paine whose bridge at Richmond (page 79) had been much admired. In the nineteenth century a floating landing stage for river steamers was constructed by the central span. (Photo from Chiswick Public Library)

The third Kew Bridge today. By the 1890s the increased traffic made the widening of Kew Bridge imperative, but it was found that rebuilding would be both safer and cheaper. The present bridge, designed by Sir John Wolfe Barry, was begun in 1899 and opened by King Edward VII on 20 May 1903. Through the bridge can be seen Oliver's Island and the Kew railway bridge (built 1864–9).

The herbarium of Kew Gardens. The house in the centre of the April 1899 photograph (above) was built in the late 1720s or early 1730s. In 1820 Robert Hunter sold it to King George IV who had plans – aborted for lack of funds – to replace Kew Palace with a new palace. The house was occupied by the Duke of Cumberland (who became King of Hanover in 1837) from 1830 until his death in 1851, when Queen Victoria presented it to the Royal Botanic Gardens as a library and herbarium. The new wing built at the back in 1876 is barely visible in the 1899 photograph, but in 1902 another new wing was added on the west side as can be seen in the present-day photograph below. (A third wing was added in 1930.) Note how the trees have grown in one hundred years.

Pagoda Vista, Kew Gardens, *c.* 1910 and 1999. In 1840 Queen Victoria agreed to the transfer of the royal gardens at Kew and Richmond to public ownership, and in 1841 Sir William Hooker was appointed as the first director of the Royal Botanic Gardens. Within a few years the original small botanic garden had been expanded almost to its present size, the great palm house had been built and a long-term plan for a new layout adopted. This included a vista, 2,800 feet long, from the palm house to the pagoda (built by Sir William Chambers for Princess Augusta in 1761–2). In 1862 the temperate house was built on the west side of the vista. A double line of young trees was planted down the centre in 1908–9, while some larger trees were transplanted to form outer lines, as may be seen in the upper photo. Today those young trees have matured into a splendid avenue (below), although many of the older trees have been lost. The temperate house was restored between 1978 and 1982.

The north side of Kew Green. The 1903 photograph (above), taken from the ramp leading up to the new bridge, shows the whole row of houses from the herbarium on the far left up to no. 81. Most were at that time tea-gardens or restaurants. The Rose and Crown pub at no. 79 had been on this site since 1730. The present-day picture (below) shows trees, largely obscuring the houses, and cars parked along every foot of roadside. But as in 1903 the only moving traffic is a solitary cyclist. Though there has been little change in the houses the view was altered considerably by the rebuilding of the Rose and Crown in mock-Tudor style, much further back from the road and leaving a garden in front.

The King's Arms and the foot of Kew Bridge, *c.* 1898. The King's Arms pub was built in 1773. The two houses on its right dated from about 1850. The rise in the roadway for the bridge began only beyond the edge of the Green. On the right is a horse tram at its Kew Bridge terminus. The service from here to the Orange Tree in Richmond ran from 1883 to 1912. On the far left is the early eighteenth-century Capel House. (Private collection)

The approach to Kew Bridge from the Green, 1998. To allow an easier gradient on to the new bridge the ramped approach now begins from about the middle of the Green. The two houses between the King's Arms and the bridge were demolished in 1899 to enable a temporary wooden bridge to be built. The pub was rebuilt in mock-Tudor style a few years after the opening of the new bridge – and now it has even lost its old name.

The old forge at the foot of Kew Bridge, 1899. There was a house here by 1726. It had become a forge and farrier's shop by 1841 and remained so until 1900. (There is no truth in the story that it was the original Rose and Crown alehouse.) The cottage next door (*c.* 1820) housed a shop and tea-room in the 1890s.

The foot of Kew Bridge today. The picturesque but ramshackle old forge was demolished when the new bridge was built. The cottage next door, despite alterations, is still recognisable in the present workshop. The bridge approach road is well above ground level here.

The Queen's School and the Kew Green pond. Originally a medieval fishpond belonging to St Swithin's Priory in Winchester, the pond was fed by an inlet directly from the river. When the Kew meadows were enclosed in 1823 Miss Elizabeth Doughty (of The Priory) gave a parcel of her allocation on the north side of the pond as a site for a new village school. The school was opened in 1826 and George IV commanded that it be named the King's Free School. It became the Queen's on Victoria's accession. The original small gothic building was replaced in 1877 by the three-storey edifice seen here. In the meantime the pond had been enclosed by a brick wall and was linked by a culvert to the river inlet, which became a small dock. (Private collection)

The Kew Green pond today. In 1970 the Queen's School moved to more spacious new premises in Cumberland Road and about 1975 a small terrace of houses was built on its site. The pond is still connected to the river through the culvert (the top of which is just visible), but the dock has now been built over. Some planting has restored a more rural appearance to the pond.

St Anne's Church, Kew Green, *c.* 1875 and 1998. The first church at Kew was a chapel built by private subscription. Queen Anne gave land on the Green and the chapel, dedicated to St Anne, was consecrated on 12 May 1714. It was enlarged in 1770 (when it became a parish church) and again in 1805, 1822–3 and 1834. In 1851 the east end was extended to provide a mausoleum for the Duke of Cambridge, leaving the church as it appears in the photograph of about 1875 (above). The entire eastern end of the church was again rebuilt and enlarged in 1884. As seen today (below), the west end dates from 1834, the south wall (now cleaned of the ivy beloved by Victorians) from 1805 and the east end from 1884. In the foreground stands the Kew war memorial.

The Coach and Horses Hotel, Kew Green. About 1770 the Coach and Horses moved from its original site at nos 11–15 on the south side of the Green to a new building on the east side. A comparison of the mid-nineteenth-century watercolour (above) with the present day photograph (below) shows a few changes, but the 1770s structure is clearly recognisable.

The inn sign still stands on the little island between the roads, but the pleasant prospect is somewhat marred by all the bollards and traffic signs. On the right, Victoria Cottage (built in the 1840s) and Richmond House (*c.* 1757) still stand. The latter was rented for some twenty-years by the Duke of Cumberland before he was given Hunter House (see page 9).

The south-east corner of Kew Green, 1928 and 1998. In 1937 the junction of Kew Road and Mortlake Road was widened and the old buildings, dating from about 1700, on the corner of the south side of the Green were demolished. They were replaced by the row of shops (now a wine bar and restaurant) seen in the present-day photograph below. Beyond the corner can be seen the first houses in Kew Road (this end of which was formerly called Richmond Road), built about 1774. They still remain, as do the shops of Mortlake Terrace, just visible on the left, built in the early 1870s. The modern photograph emphasises the traffic, now an almost continuous stream across Kew Green from the bridge to this corner.

CHAPTER TWO

PARKSHOT & KEW ROAD

The street called Parkshot derives its name from the Park Shott of the lower Richmond field, so called because it bordered the park created by James I (now the Old Deer Park and part of Kew Gardens). The footpath from Richmond Green to the Kew ferry was known as the 'foot lane' to Kew in distinction from the 'horse lane' – now Kew Road. Its northern part, nicknamed Love Lane, was taken into the royal estates in 1785, and in the nineteenth century what was left was renamed Parkshot at its southern end and Kew Foot Road at its northern. The two sections of road were divided by the construction of the Great Chertsey Road in the early 1930s.

Development started along the Kew foot lane in the 1720s. Typical of the period were 7–10 Parkshot seen in the above photograph of the 1890s. Nos 7–9 were demolished in 1900. From 1855 to 1859 no. 8 had been the home of the author George Eliot.

Kew Road, widened and improved at the expense of George III in the 1760s, was not built up much beyond the Orange Tree pub until the early nineteenth century. With the arrival of the railway in 1846 development proceeded rapidly, and after the opening of Kew Gardens station in 1869 the east side of the road was soon built up all the way to Kew.

The Guardians' Office, Parkshot, 1910. The eighteenth-century houses at 7–9 Parkshot were replaced in 1905 by a new office building for the Guardians of the Poor, the body that administered the poor law. No. 10 Parkshot House survived, but public swimming baths had been built next to it on the north side in 1882. When the Guardians were abolished in 1929 their offices became the Parkshot Rooms.

The Magistrates' Court, 1998. After the opening of the new swimming baths in the Old Deer Park in 1966, use of the baths in Parkshot rapidly declined. In 1972 they, together with Parkshot House and the Parkshot Rooms, were demolished, to be replaced by a new Magistrates' Court, opened in 1976. Nos 3–6 Parkshot still survive; part of no. 6 can be seen on the left.

The northern end of Parkshot. The upper photograph, taken in 1902, shows clearly in the background the sharp bend in the road where it continued into the Kew Foot Road. The buildings there were demolished when the Chertsey Road was built, and everything around the junction of Parkshot and Clarence Street was rebuilt. On the right the old buildings have mostly been replaced by new offices (lower picture), but no. 15 and the Sun Inn at no. 17 still survive. The Sun Inn, built about 1720, was known at first as 'the Kew Foot Lane Coffee House', but became a licensed public house under the new name about 1790, after the closure of an earlier Sun tavern in George Street.

The junction of Kew Road and the Lower Mortlake Road. The construction of the Great Chertsey Road in the 1930s involved the widening of the Lower Mortlake Road and the construction of the large traffic roundabout named Richmond Circus. The upper photograph here shows the scene as it was in 1926. As can be seen in the present-day photograph below, all the houses on the east (right) side in the earlier picture were demolished, as was the large shop at the road junction. In the 1926 picture a pair of white gables can be seen in the Lower Mortlake Road – gothic-style cottages built in 1853. One alone survived. The grassy sward in the foreground of the modern view is on the traffic island in the middle of the roundabout – the only safe place from which to take a photograph nowadays!

Shops in the Kew Road, 1926. Everything in this picture to the right of the Players' cigarettes advertisement (the sailor's head visible on the wall just to the right of the tree) was swept away to construct the new roundabout in the 1930s. John Perring's shop at the corner of St John's Grove was 71 Kew Road. Perring started as a furniture dealer in Paved Court in 1895 and expanded his business into a large chain of furnishing stores.

The Kew Road roundabout (Richmond Circus), 1998. The garage and petrol station which had occupied the corner between Kew Road and the Chertsey Road since the construction of the roundabout were replaced in the 1980s by the office building housing the European headquarters of Pepsi-Cola. The hamburger advertisement is on the same wall as the Players' one of seventy years earlier.

Kew Road by the Orange Tree, 1890 and 1995. The Orange Tree pub was rebuilt in or about 1898. The old building was on the right just outside the 1890 photograph, but the rebuilding took in also the stationery shop next door. The long low building to the left which has survived, though losing its attic windows, dates from about 1720 and was once the White Lion tavern. Further left, Crescent Terrace of eight shops, built in 1879, has now been replaced (for the second time) by an office building called Parkshot House, seen under construction in the 1995 photograph. The rails of the tramway to Kew can be seen in the road in the 1890 picture. The growth of the trees in a hundred years made it necessary to take the modern shot in the winter.

The Crescent, Kew Road, *c.* 1900 and 1998. The curve in Kew Road gave this section the name of the Crescent – no longer used. On the left in the old picture is the Station Hotel (now the Bull and Bush), built in 1877, then Crescent Terrace, a parade of shops built in 1879. Further on in the early view can be seen the tower of the rebuilt Orange Tree pub. On the right was the terminus of the railway line constructed in 1869 which ran up through Kew to Gunnersbury and Willesden, and which was later linked to the District Railway at Hammersmith. The present-day photograph shows the new office buildings which have replaced Crescent Terrace and the corner of the new station built in 1936–7.

Richmond railway station. Both views were taken from the Church Road bridge. In the upper one, dating from the 1880s, the through tracks of the London South Western Railway are on the left, but the main part of the LSWR station is out of sight beyond the Kew Road bridge. On the right is the terminal station, built in 1869 and enlarged in 1877, also belonging to the LSWR but used for the District and North London services. A District locomotive, fitted with a special condensing system to reduce the emission of steam in the tunnels, can be seen. The Station Hotel and Crescent Terrace dominate the background. The present-day view shows the new station built in 1936–7 entirely surrounded by later office buildings. A down train from Waterloo halts briefly on the left, while Silverlink (ex-North London) and District trains wait to depart.

No. 12 Waterloo Place. Waterloo Place was built about 1815 and named in celebration of the great victory. George Bliss established his chimney sweep's business at 12 Waterloo Place about 1890, later adding 'and Son' (as seen on the sign painted on the wall). His son Frederick later occupied the cottage next door, no. 11. Much of the charm of the old photograph lies in the two lanterns: the public street lamp mounted on a bracket from the wall on the right, and Mr Bliss's own above his front door, crested by a sweep's brush.

As the 1995 photograph shows, there is still a street lantern but the present one is not quite as ornate as its predecessor. The houses in Waterloo Place have been smartened up, and many of their tiny front gardens are full of flowers.

Prince's Street and Waterloo Place. Despite all the new building, especially on the right, the present-day picture (opposite) retains something of the same atmosphere as that of about 1890. This may be partly due to the posed groups of youngsters, but it is also because of the almost unchanged cottages of Waterloo Place in the centre of both pictures. On the right an old timbered smith's shop and the house behind it have given way to the new block of offices. Beyond them the Richmond Arms pub (originally called the Goose and Gridiron, as a beerhouse from the 1830s to the 1850s) has also been completely rebuilt. On the left is the old fire station building (see pages 44–5).

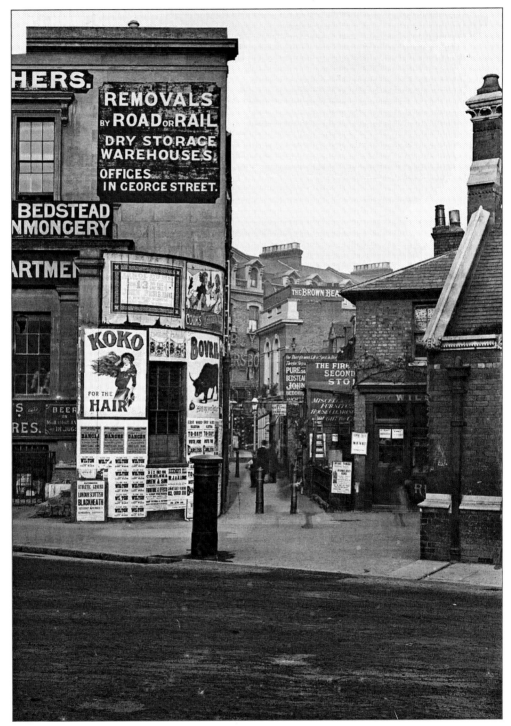

Market Passage, 1901. The building on the left, which was still domeless in 1901, is covered in the advertisement hoardings and posters that typically disfigured the urban scene a century ago. It was at this time being used as a furniture warehouse by Wright Brothers, the department store in George Street. There are almost as many posters and signboards along the passage itself.

Market Passage, 1995. On the right at the end of the passage the building of the former Brown Bear public house is recognisable, though it has now become a Next store. The Bear tavern was already established by 1703. Beyond it can be seen the shops of the Quadrant. The clutter of signs and posters has been cleared up a bit, but the fruit and vegetable stalls made Market Passage a busier, livelier alleyway.

The corner of Duke Street and the Quadrant. In 1860 (above) the buildings on the left in Kew Road beyond Duke Street were all of two storeys and stood further forward than their successors of today. Mr Trice the saddler carried on a business established early in the century by a Mr Tolley. In the white apron is Mr Gosling, an employee of Trice's. The premises with the clock and lamp were the office and waiting room of the Richmond Bus Company, and beyond them was Warner's coachbuilding workshop. These old buildings were replaced in 1877 by the long four-storeyed terrace of shops called Quadrant Buildings which still stand (see the photograph of 1995 below). These were built in line with the shops in George Street, thus widening the Kew Road. The eighteenth-century buildings on the opposite side of the road have all been replaced.

CHAPTER THREE

EAST OF THE CENTRE: LOWER MORTLAKE ROAD & SHEEN ROAD

The Lower Mortlake road from its junction with Kew Road, 1920s.

Where the road to East Sheen crossed the manor boundary into Mortlake there was anciently a marsh, so the gate at the boundary was called the Marsh Gate. What is now Sheen Road was, until the 1890s, known as the Marshgate Road. A small group of houses developed by the Marsh Gate in the seventeenth century. In the early eighteenth century the first cottages were built along the old Worple Way. Further west, at the entrance to Richmond town, stood several large mansions.

In the second half of the eighteenth century there was further development along the Marshgate Road and the first houses began to appear along the lane leading to Mortlake. In the 1820s an estate of small houses for artisans was developed on the south side of Mortlake Lane under the name New Richmond. Within a few more decades both the Lower Mortlake Road (as Mortlake Lane was renamed) and the Marshgate Road were fully built up on both sides.

The Lower Mortlake Road. The upper photograph, taken in 1932, shows the road just after its widening as part of the Great Chertsey Road project designed to provide a new main access route into London between the Bath road and the Portsmouth road. It was taken from a little further down the road than the view on page 33. The cottages on the left remained intact; on the right all the buildings facing the road and at the ends of the streets leading off it had been demolished. In the background stand the gasometers by the junction with Manor Road. Along the sides of the road a few very young trees had just been planted. These trees have now grown large, as can be seen in the present day picture (below) and the traffic has greatly increased. Hoping for a solitary motor-cyclist to match the 1932 scene, our photographer ended up with an entire squad of police motorbikes.

e Black Horse. The first building on the site of the Black Horse at Marshgate, by the corner of what are now
ieen's Road and Sheen Road, was erected about 1718 and was probably immediately leased out as a tavern
ider that sign. It had a spacious yard in front and did a good carriage trade, as the photograph of August 1904
bove) testifies. Four months after that photograph was taken Sheen Road was widened and the old, partly
nber, buildings of the Black Horse were demolished to be replaced by the rather bizarre structure that survives
day (as in the photograph below). The tree on the little island at the road junction still flourishes, and there is
ll a seat beneath it. The island replaced an original pond.

The Marshgate Arms at the corner of Worple Way and Sheen Road, *c.* 1907. Worple Way is what survives of worple or field path which divided the Upper Dunstable Shott from Marsh Furlong in the upper Richmond fie The worple originally ran all the way to the back of the Black Horse at Marshgate, and certainly pre-dated t Marshgate (or Sheen) Road, which was probably built through the strips of the Upper Dunstable Shott becau the worple was too marshy to take heavy carts. The first cottages to be built on the land between the Marshga Road and Worple Way dated from the 1720s and 1730s, but it was only about 1770 that a row of five w erected stretching right up to the point where the roads divided. The one at the apex became the Royal O beerhouse in 1862, changing its name to the Marshgate Arms about 1890. This photograph is recorded having been taken about 1907, but it may be somewhat earlier as John Bushnell, whose name appears above t door, was the licensee as tenant of the Gomm Brewery from about 1894 only to 1900. The tall buildings seen Worple Way on the right are the back of the Red Cow pub.

The Red Cow at the corner of Worple Way and Sheen Road, 1998. The clearing away of the Marshgate Arms and the adjacent cottages for road widening in 1908 left the Red Cow pub as the first building between Sheen Road and Worple Way. With its trees and potted plants it presents a far more attractive scene than the old beerhouse. The Red Cow was first established about 1725 at a site some 150 yards further east along Worple Way, on its southern side, where a little group of small buildings was developed at this time. Its landlord from 1736 to 1751 was Thomas Roberts. He purchased a piece of land with a stable between Worple Way and the Marshgate Road. His son, also Thomas Roberts, built a house on this site about 1758. Shortly before his death in 1777 he also acquired the Red Cow. In 1789 his widow Ann transferred the licence and the name to the house facing Marshgate Road, which was rebuilt, or much enlarged, to become the 'new Red Cow'. The site of the old Red Cow and the cottages around it became eventually the works of the Richmond Mineral Water & Bottling Company (a sign pointing to which is seen on the Marshgate Arms on the opposite page). The site is now that of Alberta Court.

Albert Road, 1952. The estate known as 'the Alberts' was developed to the south of Worple Way in the 1870s, though the south side of Worple Way itself was built up between 1790 and 1830. Most of the new roads were named after members of the royal family: Prince's, Albert, Albany, York, Connaught, Lorne (a son-in-law of Queen Victoria) and Beatrice – but Albert Road gave its name to the whole area. The development was of small houses for the artisan class – tradesmen and labourers. There were several beerhouses or off-licences in the Alberts, including the one at 44 Albert Road, on the right in this 1952 photograph.

Albert Road, 1998. The gentrification of the Alberts began in the 1960s. The small houses were sold off as 'suitable for renovation' or were renovated by landlords and then sold, at ever-increasing prices. No. 44 ceased to be an off-licence after 1971 and in 1978 was converted into a desirable small dwelling house, here seen gleaming in a new coat of paint.

Worple Way, north side, 1913 and 1995. Off to the left of both pictures is the Red Cow pub. With one exception the eighteenth-century cottages seen in the 1913 view (above) have been swept away to be replaced by an attractive modern building. The view is much enhanced by the silver birch tree. The sign for Watney, Combe, Reid Ales on the right of the 1913 photograph was on the rear of 71 Sheen Road, a beerhouse and off-licence that flourished from the 1870s until 1988 under the name of the Old English Gentleman.

The corner of Marshgate Road and Church Road, 1890. The Church of St John the Divine (visible in the distance) was built in 1831–6 to the designs of Louis Vulliamy, and in 1838 the former parish of Richmond was divided between the old parish church of St Mary Magdalene and St John's. A new road was developed soon after, leading off the Kew Road beside St John's up to the Marshgate Road, with groups of separately named villas. The Vestry adopted the name Church Road for the whole stretch in 1852. In 1868 Sir Charles Selwyn presented to the Vestry the land on which Church Road was then extended up the hill to St Matthias's (see page 106). By 1890 both Church Road and the Marshgate Road were built up at this corner with the same buildings that stand there today. Marshgate Road was renamed Sheen Road in 1892. Matson House (now 48 Sheen Road) on the left was in 1896 the Richmond High School for Girls. This became the Girls' County School in 1905, which was then moved to Parkshot in 1909.

The corner of Sheen Road and Church Road, 1998. The tranquil, almost rural, scene of a century ago has now become a busy intersection with traffic lights. With the introduction of one-way working and traffic bumps on Richmond Hill, Church Road has become the main road up the hill from the town centre and, with Friar's Stile Road and the Terrace part of Richmond Hill, is now the principal route from Kew to Richmond Park and an alternative route, avoiding the congestion of Hill Street and the end of Richmond Bridge, to Kingston. Matson House became a hotel in 1925 and changed its name to Quinn's in the early 1950s. About 1950 it was joined by Bishop's Hotel, on the right, at 50–52 Sheen Road. Bishop's, too, has just announced a change of name, to the Richmond Inn Hotel.

Paradise Road, 1907 and 1998. Paradise was a name often given to a churchyard, and Paradise Row (now Road) was the lane which ran from the parish churchyard to the Marshgate (Sheen) Road. Until 1853 it had a bar across it about where the haycart is seen in the 1907 picture (above). There are just two points of reference to the modern scene: the railings on the right were outside Suffield House; the building projecting forward on the left of the road was the Magistrates' Court (now Vestry House). The first buildings on the left were Eton Cottage, Suffield Lodge (with the gable) and Eton Terrace. The scene today (below) is entirely different, though Suffield House, where Leonard and Virginia Woolf set up the Hogarth Press, still stands – as does Vestry House. The rest is all new office buildings.

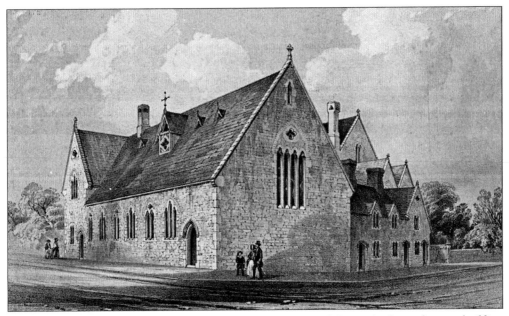

The National Schools (St Mary's), *c.* 1854. This contemporary lithograph shows the new building erected for the parish free schools when they moved in 1854 from their original site at the George Street corner of Brewer's Lane to the corner of Paradise Road and the newly opened up Eton Street. (This street was developed on church land and the vicar, who named the new road, had been a master at Eton College.) The schools had been founded in 1713. (Author's collection)

Eton House, 1998. This office block, built originally for the chemical company Bayer Ltd, after the school had moved to become part of Christ's comprehensive school in Queen's Road, is now the headquarters of the publishers Mills & Boon. It is known by some as the Lego building on account of its coloured plastic panels and general architectural style. Beyond Eton House a few recently renovated nineteenth-century cottages still remain.

The Fire Station, *c.* 1880. Following a disastrous fire at the Star and Garter Hotel, Richmond's fire brigade wa
reorganised in 1870 under a professional captain, with the firemen – still volunteers – standing by on a regula
shift basis. A new fire station, to house two engines (horse-drawn with manual pumps at that time), was built i
the Square at a cost of £700. It replaced an old two-storeyed wooden building which had served as a watch-hous
engine-house and Beadle's office. The new building had a small mortuary chapel at the foot of the clock tower an
a room above that for the firemen on duty, from which a chute provided a rapid means of access to ground leve
Before 1870 the Square could be seen as a square plot between Prince's Street and the back of the building see
on the left here. The latter started as a single-storey Mechanics' Institute in 1843, built on the site of the form
village pond. By 1880 it had acquired an upper storey and was being used as public baths and meeting rooms. (
dome was added in 1908.) On the right stood the old buildings of 'Bug Island' (see page 48). In the backgroun
large mansions still dominated this part of the Marshgate (Sheen) Road.

Sheen Road and the old fire station, 1998. A separate mortuary chapel was added on the west side of the fire station in the 1880s. The duty firemen took over the former chapel, and the chute was removed and the entrance to it on the side of the tower bricked in. The fire brigade moved to a new station in the Kew Road in 1932 and the old fire station was subsequently converted into shops. Above the shop windows can still be seen three carved stone heads, the central one representing Father Thames and the other two the heads of firemen in the brass 'dragoon-type' helmets of the 1870s. The mortuary chapel, after serving for many years as a public lavatory, has also now been made into a shop. New shops have been built round the semi-circular front of Dome Building, and a large new building stands right behind the old fire station by the entrance to Market Passage. The Square survives in name only. Beyond it are new office buildings at the corner of Prince's Street, then the Waitrose store and car park and the flats of Lichfield Court (which replaced Lichfield House in 1935). A few nineteenth-century shops survive on the other side of Sheen Road.

Marshgate Road, *c.* 1890. Except for the old fire station and the building beyond it, everything in this photograph was demolished when Sheen Road was widened. The large mansion on the right had by 1890 been divided into several houses and shops. The gatepost of the even larger Lichfield House can be seen on the extreme right. By the entrance to Prince's Street is an old blacksmith's forge. The trees on the left were in the gardens of Carrington House. The pointed roof visible to the right of the fire station belonged to the Baptist Church in Duke Street (see page 76).

Sheen Road, 1995. Though there is still a tree on the left, set into the pavement, the widening of the road has revealed the end of the row of shops at the bottom of the south side of Sheen Road. On the north side a new office block and the Waitrose store and multi-storey car park stand somewhat further back than did the buildings of a hundred years ago.

CHAPTER FOUR

THE SHOPPING CENTRE – GEORGE STREET & HILL STREET

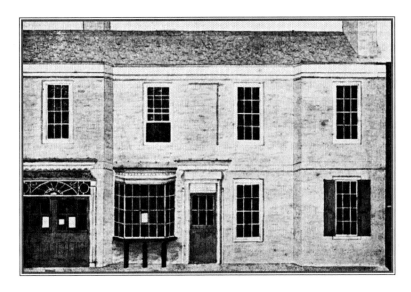

The western side of what since 1769 has been called George Street, but was formerly Richmond Street or London Street, was first developed with cottages at the rear of the larger houses facing the Green. By the end of the eighteenth century many of these had become shops and the line of building was continuous from King Street to Duke Street, apart from the entrance to Brewer's Lane. The drawing reproduced here shows William Robertson's premises at 46–47 George Street in 1838. He was a house agent.

The eastern side of the street developed somewhat later – the first houses and cottages were in the section between Hill Street and the church. There were many inns and alehouses on both sides of the street. Hill Street also had its inns and alehouses, but began to be developed with shops in the eighteenth century.

Until the town started to grow in the mid-nineteenth century these two streets, together with King Street, were the entire shopping area.

'Bug Island'. The little triangle of land at the north end of George Street, bounded by the road to Kew, the road to Marshgate and the road from the Green to the Marshgate Road, was first built on in the reign of Elizabeth I. By the late nineteenth century it had become largely a slum, known to the local inhabitants for obvious reasons as 'Bug Island'. In 1889–90 most of the ramshackle sheds and old cottages and shops were cleared away and replaced by imposing new buildings for the London and Provincial Bank and the Imperial public house. The photograph above shows the site of the bank in 1889, just before clearance; that below shows the bank building today – now a fashion shop. On the left of the present-day picture is the flower kiosk (see page 50).

Lower George Street. The upper photograph shows Lower George Street decorated for the coronation of King Edward VII in 1902. The row of little shops continues up to Eton Street (where there is a street light at the corner). The shops beyond, originally considered part of Lower George Street, had recently been renumbered as 1 Sheen Road and upwards. Just visible at 11 Sheen Road is the Marquis of Granby pub. Today Lower George Street has been pedestrianised and planted with trees (below) and its little shops have been replaced by two modern buildings. The one in the centre of the picture was for many years a large Woolworth's store.

The north end of George Street. In the 1904 photograph (above) a horse is drinking at the water trough by the obelisk. This and a similar obelisk at the George Street–King Street corner marked public water pumps. This pump and trough was replaced for many years by an underground public lavatory (promptly nicknamed 'Bog Island'), but the area has now been redeveloped with a small garden with seats and a flower kiosk (below). The rounded gable on the right is one of the oldest surviving pieces of building in Richmond. It was part of a seventeenth-century house which became the Castle Inn in the early eighteenth century. A second matching gable was lost when a new police station (now shops) was built about 1870. The corner of the police station can be seen in the 1904 photograph.

Looking south along George Street. In the early twentieth-century photograph (above) the new building of Wright Brothers' stores, completed in 1901, dominates the scene. On the right, the eye is caught by no. 49, rebuilt by the Lilley & Skinner's shoe-shop chain after a fire in September 1900. Beyond it is a row of eighteenth-century shop-houses. The foreground of the present-day photograph (below) is now filled by the small garden. The façade of the former Wrights' store was preserved when the building was recently converted for Tesco's. On the right the Lilley & Skinner building and two of the other shops survive, but almost everything else has been rebuilt.

The west side of George Street, looking north, *c.* 1890 and 1998. The 1890 photograph (above), taken from just beyond the end of Victoria Place (where the sunlight can be seen on the pavement), shows an earlier Wrights' store. The Wright brothers opened a draper's shop in 1877 at 61–62 George Street, then took over the premises at 51–54 George Street, seen here. In the 1880s and 1890s they began to expand on the other side of the road. Their new building there was completed in 1901 as a furniture store, while the drapery business continued at nos 51–54 until 1933. In the 1998 photograph below, only a few buildings remain recognisable. The two gabled ones on the left (which must be some of the earliest mock-Tudor houses in Richmond) are still there, but the one between them has been rebuilt. Three bays only of the former Wrights' store have survived – gleaming white in this picture. At the far end of the street, the Brown Bear (now Next) and Dome Building are identifiable. On the right everything visible here has changed.

The east side of George Street, looking north, *c.* 1900 and 1998. The Greyhound Hotel on the right was rebuilt and renamed (it had previously been the White Horse) about 1725. It was the main inn in Richmond's town centre until overtaken by the Castle in Hill Street in the nineteenth century, and it remained a hotel until 1923. Restored in the 1980s as a business centre, it still has an access through the old coach entrance, but shops have replaced both its main front door and its tap room. Beyond it, Williamson's grocery store survived until about 1960. The façade only of Wrights' store remains in the new Tesco building (the dome on Wrights' with its spire was a wartime casualty). At the end of the street new trees soften the present view (below).

Traffic in George Street. The photograph of 1912 (above) shows how the development of the motor bus brought visitors to Richmond in their thousands. On the left is Goslings' department store, which was replaced by the new Dickins & Jones store in 1970. The tall chimney visible in the background of the 1912 picture belonged to Richmond's power station. George Street is now one-way, and rather more filled with pedestrian shoppers than with buses on a summer afternoon. On the right nearly all the buildings, except the first one, are new; on the left a few that were in the 1912 picture can still be recognised in the 1995 photograph below.

The corner of George Street and King Street, early 1900s. By the time this photograph was taken the water pump obelisk at this corner (see page 50) had been replaced by a lamp-post, still in the middle of the road. In the later seventeenth century almost all the north side of King Street was filled with inns and taverns. One of these, the Queen's Head, rebuilt in 1854, survived until 1960 when it was taken over by Goslings' store. On the left is part of the building, demolished in 1908, of the former Feathers Inn and next to it is the Old Ship pub. It has been licensed premises (originally called the Six Bells) for well over three hundred years.

King Street, 1995. This view shows a little more of the far end of King Street where seventeenth- and eighteenth-century properties still survive. Goslings' was severely damaged by fire in the 1960s and the premises were rebuilt as Dickins & Jones store in 1970.

Looking up Hill Street, *c.* 1900. The White Hart pub on the corner of Water Lane and, immediately beyond it, t̶
Maids of Honour pastry shop were housed in buildings erected in 1696 – and the businesses were establish
almost as early. The White Hart certainly existed by 1724, by which time the second generation of Bul
pastrycooks was already occupying the house next door. The Bullens are generally credited with having f
produced the little cheese-flavoured tartlets called 'maids of honour' according to a secret recipe. The shop, r
until 1911 by three successive dynasties of pastrycooks, Bullen, Burdekin and Billett, continued to sell its special
until 1957. Set back, and barely visible, is the early eighteenth-century mansion at 5 Hill Street, which becam
the New Royalty Kinema in 1914. Later renamed the Gaumont, it was restored as offices in 1987. The clock a
part of the façade of the Town Hall can be seen beyond nos 7–9; beyond are the two terraces of shops on each s
of the entrance to Heron Court – Clarence Terrace, built in the 1690s and Royal Terrace (1838).

ooking up Hill Street, 1999. Not much of the scene of a century ago is recognisable here. On the left the omplete rebuilding of the corner of Red Lion Street has left a much wider roadway. On the right the White Hart ub was closed and became Farrow's Bank in 1915. The old building was replaced by one with rococo panels ecorating the corner. Next to it, the Maids of Honour shop closed in 1957, its business removed to Newens' akery in Kew. The shopfront was removed for preservation, but all except the overdoor glass panel has been lost. he remainder of the façade of this building has undergone only small changes. The restored no. 5 is visible only s a rooftop; no. 7 has been rebuilt, and no. 9 – the former bank (see page 60) – is just discernible. Although part f the Old Town Hall building can be seen clearly, its clock is now on a much smaller bracket and is hidden from iew. Beyond the Town Hall all is completely changed, where the new neo-Georgian blocks of the Riverside)evelopment stand in place of the former seventeenth- and nineteenth-century shop terraces.

The corner of Hill Street and Red Lion Street. The view here has altered so completely that for a change a striking night-time modern photograph (below) is contrasted with the daytime one of about 1900 (above). In both, the shops on the left occupy the site of the former Red Lion Inn, Richmond's principal hostelry from the mid-sixteenth century until the 1730s. Bletsoe's chemist's shop business (on the right) was continued by Messrs Morrell and Howells; after Morrell's death in 1955, the premises were acquired by the Council and rebuilt to widen the awkward corner into Hill Street. Further rebuilding in the 1990s as Waterstone's bookshop made the roadway even wider and allowed the construction of a pedestrian island at this busy corner.

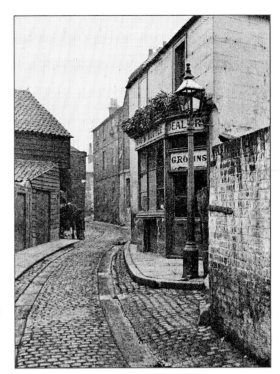

Red Lion Street, 1900 and 1998. Red Lion Street was originally a path beside a little stream leading from the churchyard to the back of the Red Lion Inn. Even when it was built up in the eighteenth and nineteenth centuries it remained a narrow winding lane (upper picture), and by the end of the nineteenth century much of the property along – and just off – it had degenerated into slums.

In 1909–12 all the old buildings were swept away and the street was straightened and widened. The new police station was built in the early 1920s on the site of the three-storey buildings seen in the old photograph, followed by the terrace of shops beyond it, and in 1926 by the Temperance Billiards Hall, which is now a four-screen Odeon cinema (below). Red Lion Street is now as full of traffic as George Street, both being one-way.

The lower end of Hill Street, *c.* 1900. The plain side wall and classical façade of the building which housed bot
Ellis's wine business and the London and Provincial Bank, with an assembly room on the upper storey, dominat
the left side of this picture. On the near side of it is the new town hall building with its protruding clock, and o
the far left the furniture shop is the first of the row called Clarence Terrace, established in houses that were bui
in the 1690s. Beyond the bank building the Spread Eagle pub stands out. It was opened in 1761 as the King
Arms, as a taproom for the Castle Hotel. In 1823 its management was separated from that of the hotel and i
name was changed to the Spread Eagle. It closed in 1909 and was converted into a shop. The vista is closed by th
old building which was once the Feathers Inn, one of the principal hostelries of seventeenth- and early eighteenth
century Richmond, which was turned into shops and offices when it was closed down about 1780. On the right
a plethora of shop signs typical of this period, and much enhanced by a wonderful pair of street lanterns outsid
the restaurant in the foreground.

The lower end of Hill Street today. Both Town Hall and bank were severely damaged by bombing in the Second World War. The former was repaired; the latter rebuilt. The vine, planted in 1840 outside the wine merchant's store, miraculously survived both bombs and builders and still grows. Appropriately the bank has now become a pub and wine bar. To compensate, the Spread Eagle has become a fashion shop. Beyond, the corner with George Street was widened up by the demolition of the old Feathers building in 1907. Shops were built in its place, but standing much further back. These were in turn replaced by a new post office in 1980 – the brick building with white stone banding in the centre of the photograph. To its right is a glimpse of the corner of the Dickins & Jones store. On the right, despite new fascias and signs, there is little change to the buildings. Thanks to the mounted police, even modern photographs can include some horses.

Richmond Town Hall, June 1893. Richmond became a Borough on 16 July 1890. In anticipation, two years before, Sir John Whittaker Ellis, Member of Parliament and former Lord Mayor of London, had purchased the recently closed Castle Hotel, which had once been owned, together with the Star and Garter, by his father James Ellis. He presented it to the town as a site for the new municipal building. The new Town Hall, designed by W.J. Ancell, was opened by the Duke of York (later King George V) in June 1893. This is how it looked then. The new side road off Hill Street was named Whittaker Avenue.

The 'Old Town Hall' today. The Town Hall was gutted by incendiary bombs in November 1940. Restored after the war, it lost most of the decorative features of its top storey. A simpler clock was placed on a smaller bracket. The building ceased to be the Town Hall when the new London Borough of Richmond upon Thames was formed in 1965 and the administrative headquarters were located in Twickenham. However, it was renovated 'for community purposes' as part of the Riverside Development project of the 1980s. Now it houses a shop (ground floor front), the tourist information office and an art gallery, the central reference library and the Museum of Richmond.

The corner of Hill Street and Bridge Street. The photograph of about 1900 (above) shows the shops of Royal Terrace built around this corner in 1838. The slightly taller building with a ground floor façade of stone was originally the entrance to a covered passage leading through to the riverside Royal Hotel. The flag is hanging from the Royal Arms pub – originally the hotel's tap room. Lower down are the Clarence Terrace shops (see page 60). All this was swept away in the Richmond Riverside Development of the 1980s (see page 87). On the right the top end of Hill Street had already been widened about 1930, when the former Talbot Hotel building, on the right in the 1900 picture, was demolished.

CHAPTER FIVE

RICHMOND GREEN

The village of Shene, the old name of Richmond, grew up beside the Green. The manor house, and from the fourteenth century the royal palace, stood on its south-west side. A royal park was created on its north-west side in the fifteenth century. Along the south-east side were the houses of the principal land-owning tenants of the manor. Although much of the palace was destroyed in the 1650s, the end of the seventeenth century and the early eighteenth century saw many of these houses (and part of the palace site) rebuilt with elegant town houses and the development of the north-east side with mansions for the rich and the noble.

In 1765 a new theatre was built at the western corner of the Green. It was opened with a prologue specially written by the famous actor David Garrick. Although small, it was pronounced 'a model for theatrical architects'. Under royal patronage it took the name Theatre Royal. One of its actor-managers, who died in 1833 in his little house (ivy-covered in the picture) attached to the theatre, was the great tragedian Edmund Kean. In the second half of the nineteenth century the theatre declined. The photograph of about 1880 shows a poster for 'Female Christys' – quite a come-down from Kean's renowned portrayal of Shakespeare's Richard III.

On the left of the picture is Wentworth House, rebuilt in the 1860s to the plans of Henry Laxton.

Garrick House in 1939. The Theatre Royal was demolished in 1884 and much of its site was used to widen the road at the corner of the Green and at the entrance to Old Palace Lane. With its disappearance, a large new house was built next to Wentworth House, on the corner of the site of the Tudor palace. It was named, evocatively, Garrick House.

Garrick Close in 1998. Garrick House was in turn replaced by a small development of houses, named Garrick Close, in 1962. Wentworth House still stands on the left of the picture.

The Palace Gateway, 1900 and 1998. One of the few surviving parts of the palace built by Henry VII in 1497–1501 is the gateway from the Green and the gatehouse adjacent to it. In the 1900 photograph (above) the diaper pattern of the Tudor brickwork is very noticeable. The obtrusive oriel window above the gate was a nineteenth-century addition. In the background, through the gate, can be seen Trumpeters' House, built in 1703–4 on the site of the former Middle Gate of the palace. The oriel window was removed and replaced by three windows and the stonework of the gate was repaired in 1939. The arms of Henry VII were renovated in 1976. Clearance of the shrubs outside the gate has revealed (lower picture) the postern gate beside the main carriage gate.

Old Palace Place and Old Friars, *c.* 1916 and 1998. Two distinguished houses at the southern corner of the Green stand in the place of five sixteenth- and early seventeenth-century houses. Old Palace Place on the left (now divided into two residences) was refronted about 1692, but the back rooms of the three old houses from which it was created still survive. Next door, Old Friars had a wing added at the rear in 1687 and was then rebuilt in front, from two old houses, in 1701–2. The two-storey wing on the right probably dates from the 1770s. During the First World War Old Friars was converted into a military hospital. It then expanded into Old Palace Place (at that time called Abbotsdene). When a door was cut between the two a painted plaster panel forming part of the outer wall of an early seventeenth-century house was revealed and removed. It is now in the Museum of Richmond.

The corner of Old Palace Terrace and King Street. Vertue Radford, the attorney for whom Old Palace Place was refronted, financed the speculative development of Old Palace Terrace about 1690–92. The houses, on the left in these views, were designed and built by the local builder William Wallins. The end bay (with a door on to King Street) appears to have been an afterthought, added very soon after the original construction. In the photograph of November 1901 (above) Mr Lloyd senior, the proprietor of the chemist's shop at 1 Old Palace Terrace, is seen at his door. The first house on the right, Oak House, with a prominent Doric porch, was built as an annexe to Old Palace Place in the mid-eighteenth century. Beyond it the house at no. 17 and the shops in King Street have seen little alteration in the last century, but those in George Street in the background have all been rebuilt (lower picture).

Paved Court, 1902 and 1995. The development in 1690–2 of Old Palace Terrace included the building of a row of shops at the rear with a passageway between the Green and King Street, then called 'the paved alley'. The shops were on the east (left in the picture) side of the alley. The western side was built up later in the eighteenth century. The main difference between these pictures is nothing structural but the smartening up of the alley into a chic shopping lane. The Prince's Head pub on the left started life as the Duke of Ormonde's Head about 1705. When Ormonde, a popular local hero but a Jacobite, fled into exile in 1715, it became the Duke's Head, changing to the Prince's Head in the late eighteenth century.

Pensioners' Alley, looking towards the Green, 1899. Another of Richmond's lanes was Pensioners' Alley (perhaps built originally to house pensioners from the palace staff). It had a row of cottages all along its north (right in the picture) side and a square courtyard (Golden Court) faced by cottages in the middle of its south side. The entrances from the Green and from George Street were both through archways beneath buildings. By 1899 most of the buildings seen in the photograph were commercial premises: a printing house on the right, the back of a George Street greengrocer's and a candle factory on the left.

Golden Court, 1998. Pensioners' Alley has been entirely reconstructed and given the name Golden Court. On the left is part of the new building of Dickins & Jones' store. The entrances were opened up, so there is now a view through to the Green.

Nos 11–20 The Green, 1903. With few exceptions these houses on the Green all date from the eighteenth century. On the left, nos 11 and 12 (with no. 10, out of the picture) were built between 1705 and 1715 on the site of the former Cross Keys tavern. Their cornices and doorcases have some of the finest architectural carving surviving in Richmond. Beyond no. 12 is Brewer's Lane, the oldest of the lanes leading off the Green, which had at least four shops in the time of Elizabeth I. Further to the right, the house with the pediment (no. 17) was built by the local architect and developer John Price about 1710 and was Richmond's leading coffee house for most of the eighteenth century.

Nos 11–20 The Green, 1998. The present-day photograph shows little change, except for the restoration of Georgian-style glazing bars in place of the large Victorian sash-window panes and the replacement of ivy on some houses with wisteria on others. Here, even an old lamp standard has been spared. But it is difficult to recapture the mood of eighteenth-century Richmond when the foreground is a solid row of parked cars.

No. 1 The Green, 1899 and 1998. No. 1 The Green (and the shop on the Duke Street frontage) is one of Richmond's oldest buildings, but there is no truth in the legend that Shakespeare stayed there. The house appears to have been built in the late 1660s to replace a cottage and shop which dated from the 1590s.

The house has changed little externally since the seventeenth century, except for the addition of the porch and a parapet and the rebuilding of the chimneys – and the creation of the shop in the 1890s. In 1899 Beard's Richmond Cycle Stores (upper photo) gave good value, catering to the new craze for cycling. Today the Buddhists (below) aim for higher values.

The Richmond Theatre. Following the demolition of the Theatre Royal in 1884 an attempt was made to use the Castle Assembly Rooms as a theatre, but after a few years the proprietor, Mr Frederick Mouflet, decided that the facilities were too restricted. He acquired a site on Little Green and commissioned Frank Matcham, the leading theatre architect, to design a new theatre. It was opened on 18 September 1899. The upper picture shows it at that time. The cannon on the Green was a Russian one, captured in the Crimean War. Renovated and enlarged a little in the 1980s, Richmond Theatre continues to mount first-rate performances. (The growth of the trees on Little Green made it necessary to take the new photograph – below – in winter rather than summer!) The leafless trees reveal the public library building to the left of the theatre and, on the right, Onslow Hall (built as a Cavalry College in 1857 after a fire had destroyed the former building of Richmond Academy). Onslow Hall now houses offices of Barclay's Bank.

Duke Street by night, 1950s. Duke Street, originally Duke's Lane, was named after Mr William Duke who owned a large mansion on its north side in the early seventeenth century. The large stone building in gothic style on the left is the Baptist Church built in 1880–1. Facing it, with a lantern hanging above the pavement, is the Cobwebs pub, which was the Coffee House tavern in the eighteenth century. Lavell's confectionery shop in the background was in the only building on 'Bug Island' (see page 48) not rebuilt in 1890.

Duke Street by night, 1999. The gothic Baptist Church was replaced by a new building in 1961–2, and that last corner of 'Bug Island' was recently rebuilt as the Monsoon shop. There has been little change externally to the buildings on the south side of Duke Street (on the right), but the Cobwebs has changed its name to the Racing Page and a new pub, the Flicker and Firkin, has opened up in the courtyard just off the far end of the street.

The interior of Richmond public library. Richmond parish council was one of the first local authorities in the London area to establish a free public library. It was built on a vacant site beside Little Green in 1881 to the designs of the town surveyor, F.S. Brunton. The upper photograph shows part of the interior in 1885. Since the central reference library was moved into the Old Town Hall in 1987, the building on Little Green has been used entirely for the lending library. There is a marked difference in the atmosphere today (below): the serious and rather forbidding interior of the 1880s has become 'user-friendly' – some might even use the word 'florid'!

CHAPTER SIX

THE RIVERSIDE & PETERSHAM ROAD

The river, with all the open spaces along its banks, and its bends and islands, is not just a beautiful setting but is one of the principal features that make Richmond such a desirable place to live. The bridge which was built across it in the 1770s to the design of James Paine is a particularly handsome one which enhanced the view. It has been the subject of innumerable paintings. Above is the earliest known photograph of the bridge, taken by the Richmond artist and photographic pioneer George Hilditch about 1855.

Although the destruction of most of the Tudor palace in the 1650s removed what had been the dominant feature of the riverside, a number of large mansions were built beside the river in the late seventeenth and eighteenth centuries – including a speculative riverside development in the 1690s that foreshadowed the major project of nearly three hundred years later.

The river was a workplace for many of Richmond's inhabitants until the early twentieth century, but it also became a place of recreation for them and for visitors – the latter especially after the railway, and later the motor bus, made Richmond more easily and cheaply accessible from London.

Richmond Bridge from Cholmondeley Walk, c. 1900. This photograph corresponds closely with the one on the previous page, taken almost fifty years earlier. The main differences observable (from left to right) are the removal of the brewery chimney in Water Lane, the building of Tower House by the end of the bridge, the removal (1859) of the toll houses at the Richmond end of the bridge and the presence of a pleasure steamer on the river. There are more rowing boats for hire and the commercial traffic seems to be a little heavier, but is still carried by sailing barge. There was still a barrier between the riverside footpath and the towpath, and the river bank of the latter was kept almost clear of vegetation. The island on the right, purchased by the Richmond Vestry from the Office of Works in 1873 and previously always known as the Bulrush Bed, was renamed Corporation Island in commemoration of the incorporation of Richmond as a borough in 1890. The elegant gentleman in the silk hat seems a little out of place. Had he disembarked from the steamer expecting to find someone to meet him; was he the proprietor of a business expecting an important delivery by barge; or was he just a visitor whiling away a few minutes in contemplation of the view?

Richmond Bridge, 1998. The old division between footpath and tow-path has been lost and the growth of foliage by the river bank, together with that on Corporation Island (at the far right), has partly obscured the view of the two end arches of the bridge. However, some thinning of the trees on the hill behind has revealed the tops of the Royal Star and Garter Home and of Stuart Court against the skyline. On the left Tower House shines brightly next to the new buildings of the Riverside Development. Although these are largely masked by trees, the White Cross Hotel is clearly visible. The row of boat-houses on the left belong to the houses built in 1834–5 and named St Helena Terrace. The houses have gardens on top of the boat-houses, looking out over the river. The river is quieter these days, with all its commercial traffic, except an occasional pleasure boat, gone. And few people choose to spend a day off rowing the family up and down the Thames.

Asgill House. This handsome villa was built by the architect Sir Robert Taylor for Sir Charles Asgill who was Lord Mayor of London in 1757–8. The house was finished by 1762. It had an elegant design with a wide bay in the centre and lower wings with bays on the ground floor only. In 1838 the Crown lease was purchased by Benjamin Cohen who added an extra storey on the wings and new rooms on the side away from the river. The upper photograph shows it as it was in the early twentieth century. Between 1967 and 1970 the house was restored to its original design by Fred Hauptfuhrer, the new leaseholder, and the architect Donald Insall. Richmond owes them a debt of gratitude. The photograph below might well depict the house in 1798 rather than 1998, were it not for the new wall and railings in the foreground.

The river bank downstream from the bridge. The railway trains and later the motor buses made Richmond a favourite place for a day's outing from London. To many people in the late nineteenth and early twentieth centuries this meant a day on the river. Richmond's watermen acquired great fleets of rowing boats to hire out, and boat-building and repairing businesses flourished in the riverside boat-houses. In the upper photograph (c. 1900) there are also barges tied up near the White Cross Hotel. There are still boats for hire today (below), though far fewer in number. Most of the boat-houses have gone, replaced by the terraced lawns of the new Riverside Development. The White Cross still thrives, but the view of it is almost obscured by the tree which grows beside Richmond's 'dock'. Pleasure boats are the only commercial traffic today, but there is a barge in the scene: the old college barge in the left foreground, used as a restaurant.

Water Lane, July 1903 and 1995. The narrow lane leading down to the river from the junction of George Street, King Street and Hill Street has kept some of its character, despite a few new buildings. It is still cobbled, with the inset granite 'rails' that enabled carts to come up from the wharf by the river. On the left the rear of what was the White Hart pub is now part of a shop; on the right the back of the new post office building has replaced the outbuildings of the former Feathers Inn. Further down on the right the Waterman's Arms pub survives, with a bright new sign, and several of the old houses have been smartened up.

The Castle Assembly Rooms and Hotham House. Hotham House on the right, named after an admiral who lived there in the second decade of the nineteenth century, was – with Heron House next door – a part of the riverside development of the 1690s. By the time this photograph was taken in the early twentieth century the Castle Hotel had been replaced by the Town Hall (centre right) but the long range of assembly rooms which stood alongside the hotel garden still housed a ballroom and a restaurant with a riverside terrace.

Henry's Bar, Whittaker House and the new Hotham House, 1995. The Assembly Rooms have given way to Whittaker House, the riverside terrace and boat-houses to Henry's Bar, and Hotham House to a larger new building of the same name, all part of the Riverside Development project of the 1980s, designed in a medley of neo-Georgian styles by Quinlan Terry. The Old Town Hall and Heron House were renovated as part of the project: they can be seen on each side of Hotham House.

The Palm Court Hotel, 1984. This view was taken just before the demolition of most of the old buildings in the riverside project area. It shows the entrance into Heron Court and, facing it, Heron House which had become the Palm Court Hotel. The old name was Herring Court until a mid-nineteenth century owner decided to decorate his house with large plaster figures of herons and to call it Heron House. The most famous occupant of the house was Emma Hamilton, who lived there briefly in 1809–10.

Heron Square, 1999. The red brick building in the centre is the former Heron House, built in the 1690s and preserved and renovated as part of the Riverside Development project. In the rebuilding the former entrance to Heron Court from Hill Street has been replaced by a new pedestrian entrance, through an archway under the new buildings, which is faced by the elegant tall building (seen to the left of Heron House) with another archway and flight of steps leading to the riverside garden terraces. Heron Court itself has been replaced by Heron Square, with a central fountain.

The Richmond Riverside Development. The upper photograph shows the scene in November 1959, with many of the old buildings already beginning to suffer from 'development blight'. Hotham House (which started to collapse a few months later and was demolished) and Heron House, both of the 1690s, are in the centre. They are flanked on the left by the Castle Assembly Rooms and (extreme left) the water company's headquarters in the former brewery. On the right are the former Royal Hotel (built in the 1820s) and Tower House of 1856. The Riverside Development project, carried out between 1984 and 1988 by Haslemere Estates, was designed by the neo-classical architect Quinlan Terry. It preserved and renovated the Town Hall building and – as seen below – Heron House, the façade (only) of the Royal Hotel, and Tower House. All the rest of the area was covered with separate, but mostly linked, blocks, giving the impression of individual development in a harmonious whole. The former separate gardens were made into a public open space with grassy banks and terraced walks.

Richmond Bridge in the early twentieth century. The motor car keeps firmly to the middle of the road; there is little chance of its meeting any vehicle as it crosses the bridge, especially not another motor vehicle. The charming young pedestrian smiles demurely beneath her enormous hat. On the left side of Bridge Street are Tower House (built in 1856 to the designs of Henry Laxton) and the end of Royal Terrace (see page 64). On the far side of Hill Street can be seen the Talbot Hotel, whose history can be traced back to the Dog Inn in 1702.

Richmond Bridge, 1995. The present-day photograph also has its elegant and charming young lady, carefully posed in the largest hat she could find! But it proved impossible to isolate just one single car crossing the bridge. Tower House and the adjacent façade of the former Royal Hotel were preserved in the redevelopment, other blocks of which have replaced the shops of Royal Terrace. But the 'campanile', long a landmark, is now somewhat overshadowed by the new turrets and cupolas.

Buses passing on Richmond Bridge, 1913 and 1995. The upper photograph shows how necessary was the widening of Richmond Bridge, successfully carried out in the 1930s by carefully dismantling the masonry on the upstream side, extending the piers and arches, and then replacing the original stonework. The old buses, though only just under 7 feet wide, could barely squeeze past each other. However, the pedestrians gazing at the river seem quite unconcerned. In the background are the Talbot Hotel and Barnard House, replaced in the present-day photograph (below) by a parade of shops and the Odeon Cinema, built in 1930.

Looking across Richmond Bridge towards Twickenham. The upper photograph, dating from about 1890, shows clearly the narrowness of the bridge. On the left is the entrance to Bridge House (seen to much better advantage from the river) and on the right stands the campanile of Tower House and the end shop of Royal Terrace. The traffic – two carts and two carriages, all horse-drawn – is not heavy. Our photographers rebelled over the present-day photograph. Standing in the middle of the road in daytime was just too dangerous and the resulting view was, they declared, just too dull. So they have presented instead this fascinating twilight picture, taken with a long exposure so that the passing cars are invisible save for the swathes of their headlamps and rear lights. Bridge House on the left was demolished in the 1950s and its terraced gardens have become a pleasant way down to the riverside. The obelisk, recording distances both to several points in London and to towns to the west, was designed as an original part of the bridge. It was reset on the modern brick wall.

The corner of Hill Rise and Bridge Street, *c.* 1900 and 1998. Although the viewpoint of these two photographs is slightly different owing to the widening of Hill Street, they show no change at all in the structure of the buildings in the centre. But on the left the Talbot Hotel has given way to shops and on the right Royal Terrace has been replaced by the Riverside Development. The King's Head has become Joe's. This site has the longest continuous history as licensed premises of any in Richmond. As a small alehouse called the Plough it was flourishing in 1659. It became the King's Head early in the eighteenth century and was enlarged in the 1770s and the 1830s. The row of eight shops and restaurants just beyond it in Hill Rise was built in the first decade of the nineteenth century.

The Richmond end of Petersham Road, 1902 and 1998. The scene looks towards the junction of Petersham Road and Hill Rise (seen from the other direction on page 99). The buildings in the centre of the 1902 photograph (above), which seem to tower above the rest, are in fact the backs of the houses in Hill Rise. The whitewashed cottages facing Petersham Road were called Hope Cottages; next to them, with the wide double door, was a slaughterhouse. The roadway was much too narrow for modern traffic and in the late 1930s all the buildings seen here on the right (east) side of the Petersham Road were demolished. The ones above them in Hill Rise survived until 1967, but all have now been replaced by the grassy slope and trees seen below. (See also page 100.)

Gothic House, Midhurst and the Paragon, *c.* 1920. The four houses named the Paragon (right of centre) were built in the 1720s and 1730s on land belonging to the parish church. To their right was the original site of the Blue Anchor pub, redeveloped as a private house about 1771, then much enlarged in the 1820s as Bingham House, the top of which is visible above the trees on the far right. Gothic House on the left was built about 1810; one of its first tenants was Madame de Staël. The white house in the centre was Midhurst, dating from the late eighteenth century.

The Paragon, 1998. Gothic House and Midhurst were pulled down when the Petersham Road was widened in 1938, and what was left of their sites became public gardens. Behind the empty sites can be seen the British Legion poppy factory. The Paragon and Bingham House (now a hotel) escaped demolition, but sadly another casualty was the little gazebo on the river wall.

Messum's Boatyard and the Three Pigeons Hotel, *c.* 1910. For much of the eighteenth century this site was Lewis's brewery, but it then became part of the gardens of Lansdowne House on the Hill. It was bought by the Duke of Buccleuch in 1870 and he then transferred to it the Three Pigeons pub which had previously stood on his land on the other side of the Petersham Road. Beside the pub Richard Messum developed a large boat-building and boat-hiring business. His boatyard and the long row of small boat-houses along the tow-path stand out in this picture. (Author's collection)

A car park, the Canoe Club and a burnt-out pub, 1998. Messum's boatyard building was taken over by the Richmond Canoe Club in the 1970s; the adjacent boat-house doors now merely screen a car park. The Three Pigeons was badly damaged by fire in March 1994, and this splendid site for a riverside tavern or restaurant has simply remained derelict ever since.

Buccleuch House and Gardens. The house was originally built by George Brudenell, Earl of Cardigan and later first Duke of Montagu, in 1761–2. In 1769 he bought up all the land where tile kilns had operated on the slope of the hill and added the site to his riverside grounds, linking them by a grotto tunnel under the road, which still exists. On his death in 1790 the estate passed to his daughter and her husband, the Duke of Buccleuch. The hillside grounds of Lansdowne House further enlarged the estate in 1869. In 1886 Sir John Whittaker Ellis purchased the house and the riverside grounds, while the Richmond Vestry bought the hillside grounds to become the public Terrace Gardens. Fifty years later the house was demolished to widen the Petersham Road and the riverside grounds were opened to the public as Buccleuch Gardens. Both old (early twentieth century – above) and new views here are looking towards Richmond Bridge from the southern end of the gardens.

CHAPTER SEVEN

RICHMOND HILL

The northern edge of the plateau on which Richmond Park is situated drops down as far as the line of George Street and the Sheen Road. On the west side a steep escarpment stands above the river, Petersham meadows and Ham. On the edge of this escarpment the 'upper causeway' (now Richmond Hill) was constructed to by-pass the marshy and often flooded 'lower road' to Petersham.

A very few cottages stood along the causeway in the early seventeenth century, but following the enclosure of Richmond Park in the 1630s more houses were built outside the park gates and along the road. In the 1690s and the first years of the eighteenth century some of the houses that still exist were built, a few of them on turnings off the hill such as Ormond Road and the Vineyard. The terrace walk at the top of the hill, overlooking the bend in the river, was laid out. (There had been a seat there for those wanting to admire the view at least as long ago as the 1650s.)

In the 1760s and 1770s Richmond Hill became a fashionable place to live and several new mansions were built. Then, in the mid-nineteenth century, the whole area of the hill began to be filled with new streets of detached and semi-detached villas.

The photograph above is the earliest known of the Terrace Walk, taken from outside Wick House (see page 110) in the 1860s.

The Bethlehem Chapel and the corner of Ormond Road and the Hermitage, 1900 and 1995. Ormond Passage, the narrow alley which ran down from this corner to the Red Lion pub, together with the old buildings at the corner, were swept away in the slum clearance of 1909. However, the little chapel built beside Ormond Passage for a Calvinist congregation in 1797 survived. Along Ormond Road in the 1900 picture (above) can be seen the high roofs with twin gables of the Hollies and the Rosary, built about 1697. These roofs with their wide central chimneys are still evident in the 1995 photograph below. When the grounds of The Hermitage, a house at the southern end of Church Terrace, were developed with houses in the mid-nineteenth century the new road was named after the house. (It leads off in the foreground.)

The junction of Hill Rise and Petersham Road, 1887 and 1998. Modern developments here may have improved the traffic flow, but it is far from certain that they have improved the attractiveness of the scene. All the buildings on the narrow spit of land between Hill Rise and Petersham Road as far back as Compass Hill have been demolished: the lower ones in Petersham Road in the 1930s, the rest in 1966–7. Gone too are the splendidly elaborate wrought-iron lamp-post and the stone water fountain. On the left Holbrook House (with the rounded bay) has been restored, but all the eighteenth-century houses above and below it have had shops built in what were their front gardens. Hill Rise is now a one-way street with traffic bumps, while the widened Petersham Road carries a heavy load in both directions.

Compass Hill, 1940 and 1998. *Rus in urbe*: the demolition of all the buildings north of Compass Hill, and some of those on its south side also, has turned this corner into a well-treed grassy slope with a much more countrified look than it had sixty years ago. Compass Hill derived its name from the Three Compasses alehouse which originally stood at the top corner of the hill on the south side. In 1783–4 the name was transferred to the former Rising Sun alehouse at the bottom corner on the north side. The new Three Compasses evolved into the Compasses Hotel, demolished for road widening just after the upper photograph was taken in July 1940.

The corner of Hill Rise and the Vineyard, *c.* 1900 and 1995. Shops began to develop up Hill Rise in the 1880s and 1890s, though the house at the corner of the Vineyard had been a baker's since the 1790s. Although their uses have changed in many cases, there has been little change in the buildings themselves on the right-hand side of the road in these two views. One which has not changed its use, but is now more prominent, is the Victoria pub, a beerhouse since 1851. One of the buildings opposite, demolished in 1966–7, had been until 1908 the Prince Albert beerhouse. The names probably commemorated the Great Exhibition of 1851.

St Elizabeth's Church in the Vineyard, 1908 and 1998. The first Roman Catholic chapel in Richmond since the reformation was opened in no. 1 the Vineyard in or about 1792. In 1821 Miss Elizabeth Doughty (of Doughty House, Richmond Hill, and the Priory, Kew) purchased Clarence House and the freehold close adjacent to it and then, selling off the house and some of the land, built at her own expense on the remaining plot of freehold land a new church and a house for the priest. She vested the land and buildings in trustees for the church in 1824. The church was dedicated to St Elizabeth of Portugal. It was enlarged and much altered, with a new tower added, in 1903.

Just beyond St Elizabeth's can be seen the Congregational (now United Reform) Church, built in 1831 and rebuilt to the same plan after a fire in 1851. On the right in both pictures, but showing more clearly in the modern one, are the gateposts and the wall round the front yard of Clarence House. When Nathaniel Rawlins, a London haberdasher, built the house in 1696 he was fined for 'turning the Church way'. That bend still exists in Patten Alley, the entrance to which is marked by two bollards just to the right of the lamp-post.

Cardigan House, c. 1918. Cardigan House stood on part of the site of Richmond Wells, a place of entertainment opened in 1696 in conjunction with the mineral springs found on the slopes of the hill some twenty years earlier. The Wells were closed down in 1763 and one of the remaining houses was purchased by Robert Sayer in 1776. The architect Robert Mylne supervised the building of a new house on this site for Robert Sayer in 1791–3, though the original design was not his. Sayer's first tenant from 1794 to 1797 was the Duke of Clarence. The house was purchased about 1805 by the 5th Earl of Cardigan, from whom it took its name. It was in its last years as a private residence when this picture of soldiers being entertained was taken in 1918.

Hewson Terrace, 1998. Cardigan House was acquired as a clubhouse by the British Legion in 1935, and in 1950 a large part of its grounds was sold to the Richmond Council to be added to Terrace Gardens. By the late 1960s the house had deteriorated too far to be saved and it was demolished in 1970 to be replaced by the British Legion flats named Hewson Terrace.

Friar's Stile Road, *c.* 1890. The Friar's Stile stood at the junction of field paths at what is now the top end of Marlborough Road, where a lamp-post can be seen in front of trees on the right of the picture. It was first mentioned in the manor rolls in 1649 when it was ordered that John Spicer should 'make and maintain a sufficient stile and bridge called by the name of Fryer's Stile' in return for the right to pasture his own cattle on the grass of the field path leading to it. How the name originated is, however, unknown. (The friary in Richmond owned no land apart from its own house.) The first development of any housing along Friar's Stile Road began in the 1820s and 1830s, but it was not until the 1860s that the row of shop-houses called Foxton Terrace, seen here on the right, and the large villas on the left were built.

riar's Stile Road, 1998. The first substantial building in the road was Rose Cottage, built in the 1820s, which had
a tea garden. In the 1840s it became a small hotel (much preferred by the author Thackeray to the pretentious
Star and Garter). In the 1870s its name was changed to the Marlborough Hotel. Though no longer a hotel, and
partly converted into shops, some of the premises remain as the Marlborough public house, just visible with its
lantern on the far right of this picture. Although most of the scene remains unchanged since 1890, a new row of
shops with flats above was built, to the designs of Eric Lyons, in the 1950s. (It is partly hidden by the trees on the
left of the picture.) The spire of St Matthias can be seen in the background.

St Matthias Church, 1870. As houses began to cover the upper field of Richmond and the parish lands off Queen's Road in the 1850s and 1860s the need was felt for a new church to serve this area. In 1857 Charles Selwyn, a wealthy land-owner and a churchwarden, gave a piece of land at the southern edge of his large estate, by the northern end of Friar's Stile Road. The church was designed by the famous architect Sir George Gilbert Scott and was consecrated in August 1858, though the spire was not completed until 1862. In 1868 Charles Selwyn (then Sir Charles) handed over to the Richmond Vestry the land on which a new road was made to extend the existing Church Road from Marshgate (now Sheen) Road up to St Matthias.

St Matthias and the top end of Church Road, 1998. Though restored externally and altered internally, St Matthias viewed from this side looks much the same today as it did in 1870. The clock was added to the tower in 1871. But today the nave is almost hidden by trees. Church Road was rapidly built up with substantial villas, now almost all divided into flats.

The Roebuck stables, 1850s. The Roebuck on Richmond Hill is one of the oldest Richmond pubs still trading on its original site and under its original name. It dates back to about 1720. In the above photograph its façade is partly hidden by the tree trunk but the front porch with its lantern can be clearly seen. On its north side was a building containing a coachhouse and stables; by 1850 this had been rented by the Roebuck which had developed into a small hotel. The Terrace Walk is in the foreground.

Terrace House and the Roebuck, 1998. The stable building was replaced by the imposing Terrace House in the first half of the 1860s. For some fifty years after 1875 it was the home of Sir Max Waechter, who played a leading part in the preservation of the view from Richmond Hill when this was threatened by development at the turn of the century. Between the new trees the Roebuck can be seen clearly, and next to it Terrace Cottage with its Regency balcony, then 1 and 2 The Terrace. On the left is a pair of late eighteenth-century houses, 124 and 126 Richmond Hill.

The Terrace Walk, 1890 and 1995. The scene in 1890 (above) is full of small children and prams, most of them in the charge of nannies. These days one sees as many dogs as children (below), but the benches are still full of people enjoying the view and the sunshine. On the right the tall houses of Downe Terrace, built in 1872, have become flats under the name Stuart Court – as have the houses in the somewhat later projecting block at the corner of Friar's Stile Road. The trees which in 1890 were still growing (to a great height) from the side of the roadway have all gone, but the avenue has been replanted at a lower level by the edge of Terrace Walk.

Wick House, 1930s. Built by Sir William Chambers for Sir Joshua Reynolds in 1771–2, Wick House was a plain structure of four storeys with a wide three-bay front, presenting a square façade to the road. Apart from the doorway the front was totally without ornament. The house was enlarged in the mid-nineteenth century by the addition of an extra bay with a tower on the south side. Then, during the ownership of Alexander Tod from 1861 to 1894, it was further enlarged and given a wholly Victorian appearance, as seen here. In the 1920s Wick House became a residential hotel and later an annexe of the Richmond Hill Hotel.

Wick House, 1998. Shortly before the outbreak of the Second World War a proposal to demolish Wick House and build a block of flats in its place had been approved. The house was saved by the war; the project was dropped, and the army moved in for the duration. In 1948 Wick House was purchased by the Royal Star and Garter Home and, after reconstruction which partly restored its Georgian appearance, it was opened as a nurses' home in 1950.

The Lass of Richmond Hill, March 1900. The first pub of this name was opened on the Queen's Road site in the 1840s. There is a story that John ('Jackie') Harris, its proprietor, had expected a lot of custom when he heard that a 'new college' was to be built opposite. He was disappointed to find that the students were teetotal Methodists! The pub had been rebuilt at least once before this photograph was taken, shortly before the next rebuilding.

Old Orleans, 1998. The Lass, after its rebuilding, had a more welcoming appearance. In the mid-1980s it changed its name to Old Orleans and its pub food to an Americanised menu. As Richmond College opposite had by that time ceased to be a Methodist institution and had become an international college with an American syllabus, the owners were perhaps hoping to score where John Harris had failed.

Nos 98 and 100 Queen's Road, 1960s. These were typical of the large villas built in the 1850s and 1860s along Queen's Road on the estate belonging to the Richmond Parish Lands charity. The charity arose from the grant by George III and Queen Charlotte to the Richmond Vestry in 1786 of a substantial part of Pesthouse Common, on which to build a workhouse and make a new cemetery and for the 'employment and support' of the poor of the parish. The income from this development went towards the poor rate. The coach seen in the photograph was on its way to the Richmond Horse Show. (Author's collection)

Greville House old people's home, Queen's Road, 1998. Greville House (seen here from the rear) stands on the site of 98 and 100 Queen's Road. There was a great local battle with the Council in the 1960s over how the Queen's Road estate should be redeveloped. The end results were a complete reconstitution of the charity and much new housing, a lot of it built by housing associations. Part of the land at the northern end was bought by the Council from the new trustees, as sites for a school (St Elizabeth's) and an old people's home. These, built in the early 1970s, were the first new buildings to be finished on the estate, the full redevelopment of which has taken another thirty years to complete.

The Star and Garter Hotel from the Park, *c.* 1905. The Star and Garter started as a small tavern in 1738, and had grown into an important inn by the beginning of the nineteenth century. It was greatly enlarged in the 1820s. In 1860 it was taken over by a company who in 1865 erected on its south side the extra block of accommodation seen here, designed by E.M. Barry. A serious fire in 1870 destroyed the remaining older buildings which were replaced by an enormous dining hall (with many private dining rooms also). At the end of the nineteenth century the Star and Garter was *the* place for an evening or weekend trip out of London.

The Royal Star and Garter Home, from the Park, 1998. The advent of the motor car, enabling people to travel further afield, spelled disaster for the Star and Garter, which closed in 1907. In the First World War it was turned into a home for disabled servicemen. After the war the hotel buildings were pulled down and the new Royal Star and Garter Home, opened by King George V and Queen Mary in 1924, was built in their place.

Richmond Park Gate, 1904 and 1998. The Richmond gate of the park, as seen in the upper picture, was built in 1798–9 to the designs of Sir John Soane. There was a central carriage gate, one smaller pedestrian gate and a lodge (on the right), the latter balanced by a dummy building on the left. In the second half of the nineteenth century public access to the park in the hours of daylight was progressively freed from restriction. Increasing road traffic made it necessary to widen the carriage gates. The solution adopted for the Richmond gate was to make two vehicle gates, for entry and exit, with a greatly widened carriageway. Later a third gate was opened in the centre, to divide the outgoing traffic into two streams, as seen below.

The Mansion and Star and Garter Hotels, seen from across the river, *c.* 1905. The Star and Garter is seen here on the right, with Barry's block and the dining hall block built in the 1870s. To its left and somewhat lower on the hillside is another hotel, originally called the Richmond Hill when built in 1864, but later the Mansion. Below it is the stable block of Buccleuch House. Further to the left the Wick and the houses on the Terrace can be seen on the skyline and Buccleuch House stands by the riverside at the left of the picture. (Author's collection)

The Petersham Hotel and the Royal Star and Garter Home, 1998. With the disappearance of the great Star and Garter Hotel, the Mansion for a while adopted this name, but has now been luxuriously renovated as the Petersham. The Star and Garter Home now dominates the skyline, otherwise unchanged as to buildings; but in this picture Terrace Field and Terrace House are rather more visible. Buccleuch House has vanished (see page 96) and its stables are now the Rose of York public house. In the place of the punts moored in the river in the 1905 picture there are now smart cabin-cruisers.

CHAPTER EIGHT

PETERSHAM & HAM

t the time of the Domesday survey Petersham was a separate small manor belonging to Chertsey Abbey, while Ham (like Shene and Kew) was still part of the royal manor of Kingston. Ham emerged as a separate sub-manor about 1200. In 1415 King Henry V acquired both Petersham and Ham which were then administered together with Shene (or Richmond as it became in 1501) until the seventeenth century. Ham and Petersham were granted in freehold to the Earl (later Duke) of Lauderdale in 1671.

Petersham and Kew were united into a single vicarage and parish in 1769, and after Richmond became a Borough in 1890 it absorbed this extra parish council in 1892. Ham, which had no chuch, let alone parish status, until 1831, remained as a separate unit – later an urban district council – until brought into the Borough of Richmond in 1933.

Both small villages were the sites of some large mansions built in the late seventeenth and early eighteenth centuries, many of which survive today. The villages largely escaped development until the 1920s and 1930s when new houses lined the west side of the road between them and some new streets were built at Ham. Then came major developments at Ham in the 1960s.

The photograph above, of the Dysart Arms in Petersham about 1852, is another example of the pioneering photographic work of George Hilditch.

The corner of Petersham Road and Star and Garter Hill. The upper photograph, taken in September 1904, shows a truly rural scene. As Petersham Road bends round to the left, Star and Garter Hill continues up the slope, with the wall of Richmond Park on its right. The present-day picture below shows the impact of modern transport. Traffic lights, bollards, signs painted all over the road surface, the old lamp-post replaced by new light standards five or six times the height, all speak of the volume of traffic here, building up at peak times into a slowly moving traffic jam.

The Dysart Arms, 1902. This photograph may be compared with the one on page 117, taken fifty years earlier. There had been very little change in that time – even the unusual double row of window boxes was still in place. From its origins in the early eighteenth century the pub was called the Plough and Harrow. Between 1834 and 1838 it changed its name to honour the freehold owners and lords of the manor, the Earls of Dysart of Ham House.

Café Dysart, 1998. Shortly after the 1902 photograph above was taken, the Dysart Arms was rebuilt in mock-Tudor style. It changed its name to The Dysarts in the late 1980s, and now its sign-board has changed yet again, to Café Dysart. As this legend is displayed on a shield, one cannot but wonder what was found wrong with the Dysart Arms.

The Russell British School and the entrance to Bute House, 1875. In 1852 Lord John Russell, to whom Pembroke Lodge in Richmond Park had been granted in 1846, applied for a small grant of land by the main road in Petersham Park as a site on which to build, at his own expense, a British School for Petersham. (British Schools were non-denominational.) The school remained under direct Russell family patronage until 1891. On the right of the picture are the lodge-gates of Bute House; parked outside are Victorian charabancs which had no doubt brought visitors either to the house or to the Park.

The entrance to Cedar Heights, 1998. The Russell School was destroyed by a bomb in November 1943, and was rebuilt after the war on a new site further along the Petersham Road. Bute House was demolished in 1894. In its grounds new roads and houses were gradually developed: at the southern end in the 1930s, and the northern end, with a road called Cedar Heights, only in 1967–9.

Petersham Church and Petersham House. There is little obvious change between the top picture (an early twentieth-century postcard) and the photograph of 1998 below. But there is a difference: the open footpath running across the meadow in the earlier view has been enclosed between a fence on the right and a hedge to the field in the foreground. St Peter's Church is an ancient pre-Conquest foundation, but the present fabric is mostly eighteenth or nineteenth century. Its interior still preserves the layout of 1840, with galleries and box pews. Petersham House was built in the late seventeenth century, but had an extra storey added about 1810.

The Fox and Duck, Petersham, *c.* 1909 and 1995. The Fox and Duck pub can be traced with certainty back to 1733, and possibly to about 1709. (It was not, as has been stated, previously called the Horse and Groom – a pub that was elsewhere in Petersham.) The old building (above) was demolished in 1940 and replaced by the one seen below. The small single-storey timber building to the left of the pub was the village watch-house and lock-up, which remarkably has survived to the present day, though it has been rebuilt further back. On the right of the old photograph the tower of All Saints Church can be seen in the distance. This large romanesque basilica was built in 1907–8, but was never consecrated and is now being converted into a private house.

Shops in the Petersham Road, Ham. The date of this photograph is uncertain, but is probably around the 1890s. The little group of shops, in a row called St Mary's Place, stood just south of the boundary between Petersham and Ham. Second from the right is Slades' sweetshop and further down is Hills, the bakers. Barely distinguishable on the far left are the houses called Park Place. (Photo lent by Sylvia Greenwood)

Petersham Road, Ham, 1999. St Mary's Place has gone, replaced by a double-fronted shop-house – now a photographer's studio – with an alley on the left leading to another house at the back. Beyond, however, the next two houses – their shop-fronts replaced by normal windows and a door – are quite recognisable from the scene of a century ago, as are the houses of Park Place.

The pond on Ham Common, *c.* 1900 and 1998. The view westward across the pond was much more open a century ago than it is today. From left to right in the old photograph are the early eighteenth-century Ensleigh Lodge, then the timber-framed malthouse with its louvred ventilation shaft, and Malthouse Cottage; then (to the right of the tree) St Andrew's Church school (built 1876–7 and enlarged in 1890). At the far right is Selby House, built in 1688 and enlarged some twenty years later. The malthouse and its cottage have long since disappeared but Ensleigh Lodge and Selby House still stand. So does the school building, but it has been adapted to a new use as St Thomas Aquinas Roman Catholic church and church hall. (Old photograph lent by Sylvia Greenwood)

The cottage by the south gate of Ham. Often erroneously described as a toll-gate cottage, this was one of a pair built in 1771 by the gates across the Richmond–Kingston road on the north and south sides of Ham Common. The gates were to prevent cattle straying. The cottages were used as almshouses, their occupants having the task of gate-keepers. The upper photograph (date uncertain, probably 1880s) shows Widow Morffew at her door. She was moved into the southern cottage in 1858 and lived there until her death in 1892. Notice the stand-pump on the left, one of those provided for the communal use of villagers. The northern gate cottage, by the New Inn, was demolished in 1855, but the southern one has survived to become today a solicitors' office (below).

Ham Close, 1952 and 1998. Ham Close was a short road between Woodville Road and Ashburnham Road. Immediately after the Second World War a line of 'prefabs' – the standard prefabricated emergency housing – was erected here to house people made homeless by bombing. In the 1960s the whole area was redeveloped by the Richmond Council with five-storey blocks of flats, set well apart and pleasantly landscaped. In the right foreground is the police station. The name Ham Close was extended up to Back Lane, to cover all fourteen new blocks.

Lammas lands, Ham, *c.* 1930. Charles Greenwood and his son are seen gathering asters from their flower fields, rented from the Dysarts. The Lammas lands were originally lands in which villagers were allowed grazing rights after Lammas (1 August). The rights were gradually eroded until they were ended altogether in 1958. The two buildings in the background probably belonged to Coldharbour Farm. (Photograph reproduced by permission of Sylvia Greenwood)

Part of the Wates estate, Ham, 1998. The development of the large Wates estate in Ham in the 1960s covered what was left of the Lammas lands as well as some of the huge gravel pits exploited by the Dysarts between 1900 and 1952. St Richard's Church (seen here on the right) with its adjacent school, and the Water Gypsies pub (on the left) are central features of the estate.

INDEX